Black Fathers Are Real: We Do Exist.

Written by: Jerry McRae
Illustrated by: Aaron Archie

Published by Lee's Press and Publishing Company
www.LeesPress.net

All rights reserved 2017, Except for brief excerpts for review purposes, no part of this book may be reproduced or used in any form without written permission from Jerry McRae and/or the publisher.

This document is published by Lee's Press and Publishing Company located in the United States of America. It is protected by the United States Copyright Act, all applicable state laws and international copyright laws. The information in this document is accurate to the best of the ability of Jerry McRae at the time of writing. The content of this document is subject to change without notice.

ISBN-13: 978-0999310328 *Paperback*
ISBN-10: 0999310321

Thank you for purchasing this classic children's book, a piece of the Infallible Entertainment series.

About the Author

Actor, Artist, Author, Business Owner, D.J., Father, Librarian, Motivational Speaker, Philanthropist, Professional and Writer, Jerry McRae is defined by one word, *"Success"*. A perfectionist in all that he does, he is the Founder and CEO of Infallible Entertainment, LLC, a sharp young businessman that's definitely on the path to greatness. His Charismatic personality, brilliant mind, humorous wit, engaging conversation, great smile and overall positivity is sure to make an impact on the community and the world! He has been a part of various organizations such as the drummer for UNCW's Gospel choir, Black Student Union, NAACP, and a very distinguished, handsome, successful man of the greatest fraternity on Earth, **Kappa Alpha Psi Fraternity Inc.**!! He is a new father to two amazing children, Camren Jerrimiah McRae and Brianna Keliah McRae. His excitement and joy that he gets spending with his children every moment inspired him to write this book and share the importance of black fathers.

Originally from Red Springs, North Carolina, Jerry has performed with the BIGGEST names in North Carolina, such as Saundrea Lee, Precise, B Russ, Haji P, P. Wonda, Norkotix, Shelly B, Cupid Shuffle, Maserati Fox from G Unit, etc. when it comes to music. But writing has always been a passion in his life. Writing poems through middle school and high school, Jerry took his talent seriously by enhancing his skills, attending the University of North Carolina at Wilmington. He graduated with a Bachelor's Degree in English with a double minor in Creative Writing and Biology. At first glance, he is modest, quiet and humble, but on things he's passionate about, he is very vocal, and committed to making changes for the better.

An experienced author, librarian, and businessman who is passionate about uplifting the black community. Among other things, he is passionate about positivity, development, education, and philanthropy.

Currently, the author of Black Fathers Are Real: We Do Exist is a Reference Librarian at an ACRL Excellence in Academic Libraries Award Winning Library! This book aimed at the negative stereotypes of black fathers and the assumptions that they do not handle their responsibilities as fathers. These issues happen in every race, but Black Fathers Are Real and the majority of black men DO spend time with their kids, love them, protect them, teach them right from wrong and inspire them.

www.itsinfallibleentertainment.com

About the Book

Have you ever heard the sayings, "Black Men Are Not Present in Their Kids' Lives"? The Increasing Number of Single-Parent Homes is Exclusively A Black Problem? Black Fathers Are An Anomaly?

If so, *Black Fathers Are Real: We Do Exist* is the book for you. This classic children's book conveys the importance of fathers in lives of their children. Narrated by Camren J. McRae, he specifically highlights Black Fathers, making known to the world that they do exist. Black Fathers are hardworking, educated, loving men who wants the best for their children. this book shines a light through on Black Fatherhood through Camren's eyes, the views from a child about his hero.

According to the National Health Statistics Report, Fathers' involvement in their children's lives has been shown to have a positive effect on children and their well-being in many areas. for example, on increasing the chances of academic success (2 out of 3) and in reducing the chances of delinquency and substance abuse. (4 out of 6).

According to a CNN report, statistics from the Centers for Disease Control and Prevention (CDC) reported that "children under the age of 5: Black Fathers prepared and/or ate meals more with their children vs their white and Hispanic counterparts. Children 5 through 18: Black Fathers took children to and from activities daily more compared to their white and Hispanic counterpart's. Children 5 through 18: Black Fathers also helped their kids with homework more than their white and Hispanic counterparts."

(**Source cited:** Aaron Paxton Arnold. "dispelling the myths about black fathers",

http://www.cnn.com/2015/07/20/opinions/arnold-black-fathers/index.html)

In an effort to educate, inspire, motivate, and captivate the audience, *Black Fathers Are Real: We Do Exist* is a great depiction of day to day interactions with a black father. it involves lessons learned, the culture, and the inspiration Camren receives, which is received by millions of African American children.

This book is dedicated to my son Camren and my parents, George & Nettie McRae.

Black Fathers Are Real: We Do Exist.

Hi, my name is Camren, but my friends call me "Cam"! I'm a proud African American and proud to have an African American father, but according to society, I'm wrong for my thoughts. Society places African American fathers in the same category as Iron Man or Superman, fictional, but I say they're wrong!

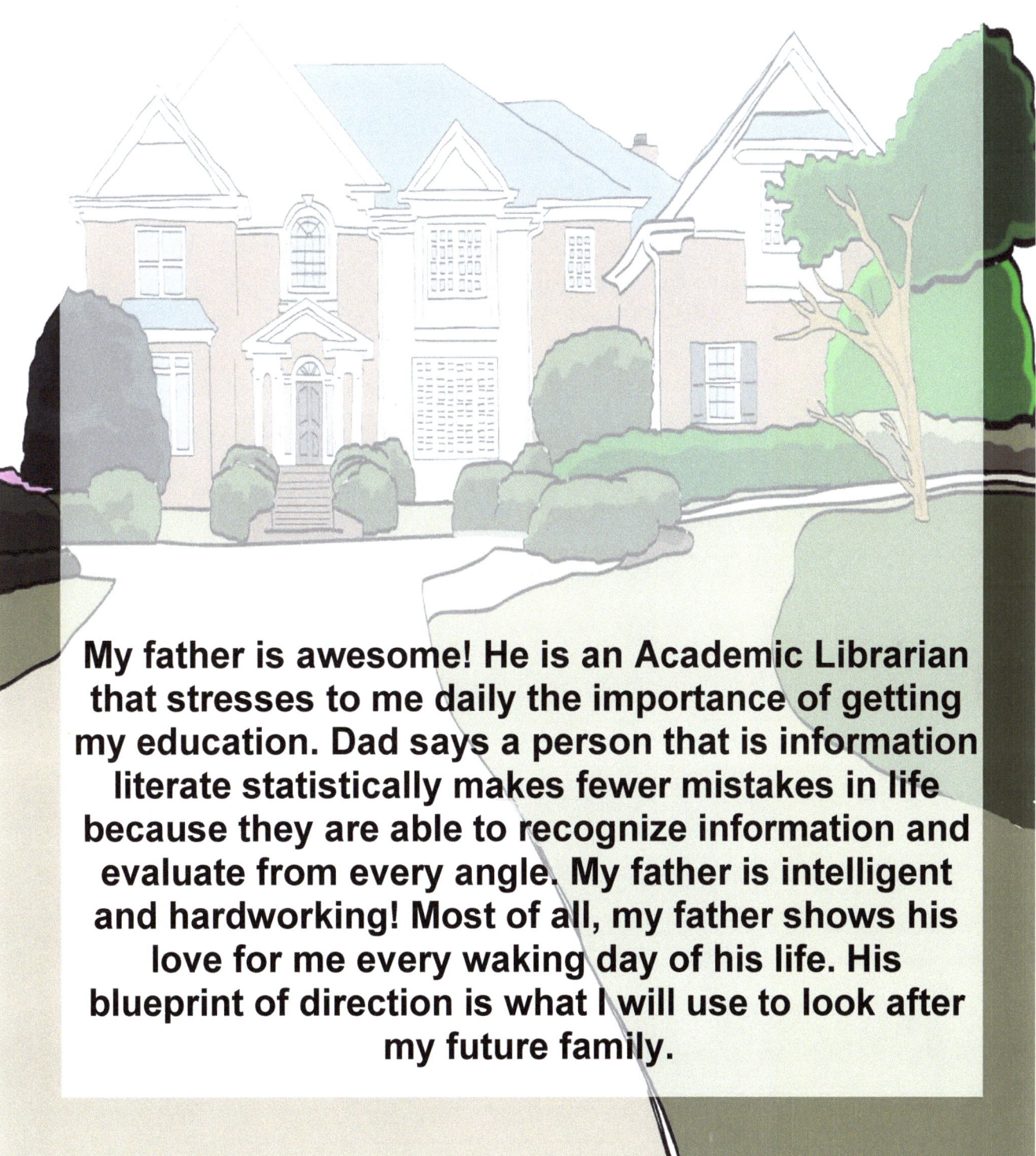

My father is awesome! He is an Academic Librarian that stresses to me daily the importance of getting my education. Dad says a person that is information literate statistically makes fewer mistakes in life because they are able to recognize information and evaluate from every angle. My father is intelligent and hardworking! Most of all, my father shows his love for me every waking day of his life. His blueprint of direction is what I will use to look after my future family.

My father, a black father, loves my mother, he cherishes my mother. He still surprises her with gifts, opens doors for her and romances her on nice dates. Mom still tells me the story of how my dad would rub her tummy as he sang to me. "Little Boy Blue, come blow your horn, the sheep in the meadow, the cows in the corn. Where is that boy, who looks after the sheep…. Under the haystack fast asleep." He's a great definition of what love is. My father goes above and beyond to make our family happy.

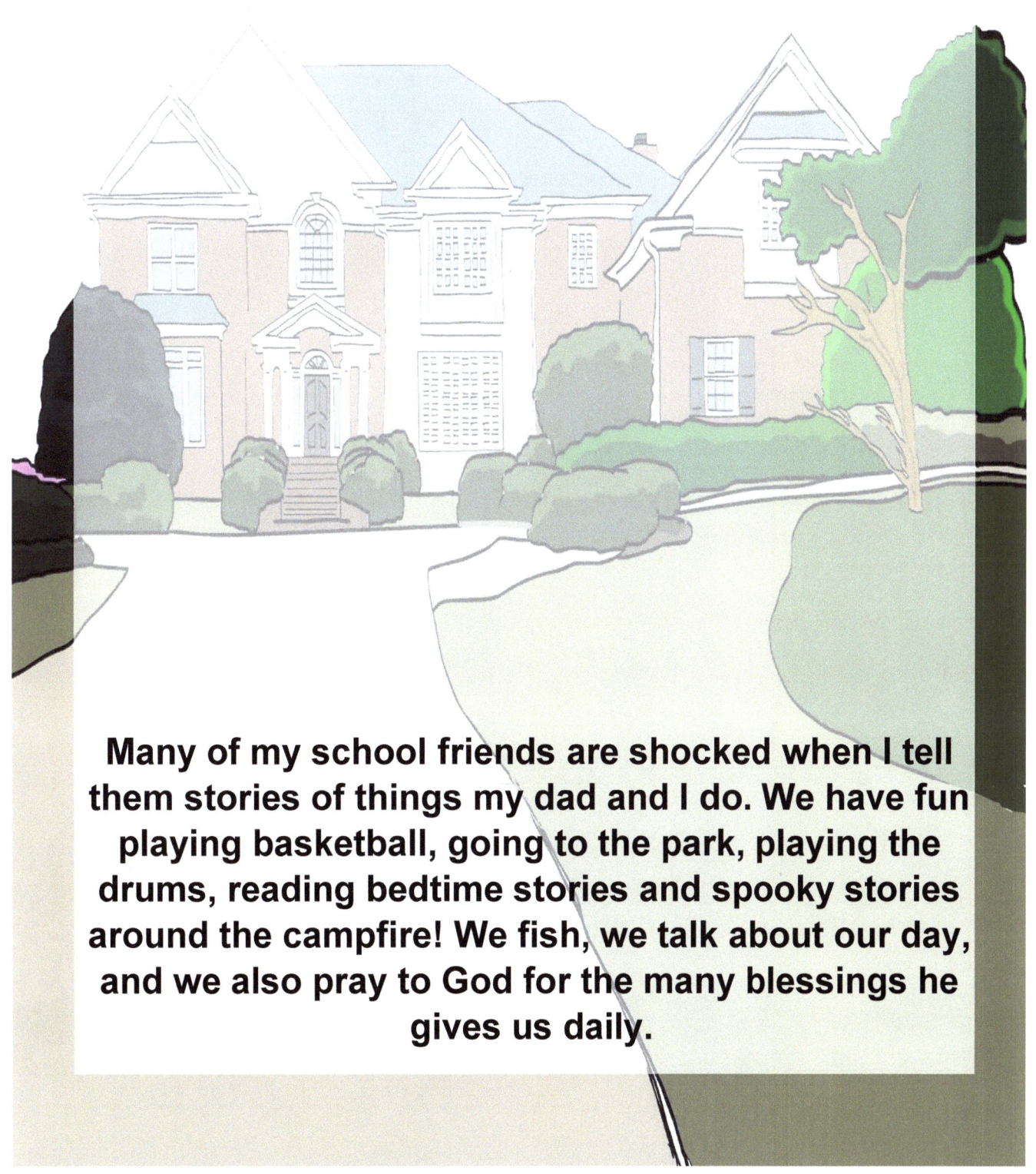

Many of my school friends are shocked when I tell them stories of things my dad and I do. We have fun playing basketball, going to the park, playing the drums, reading bedtime stories and spooky stories around the campfire! We fish, we talk about our day, and we also pray to God for the many blessings he gives us daily.

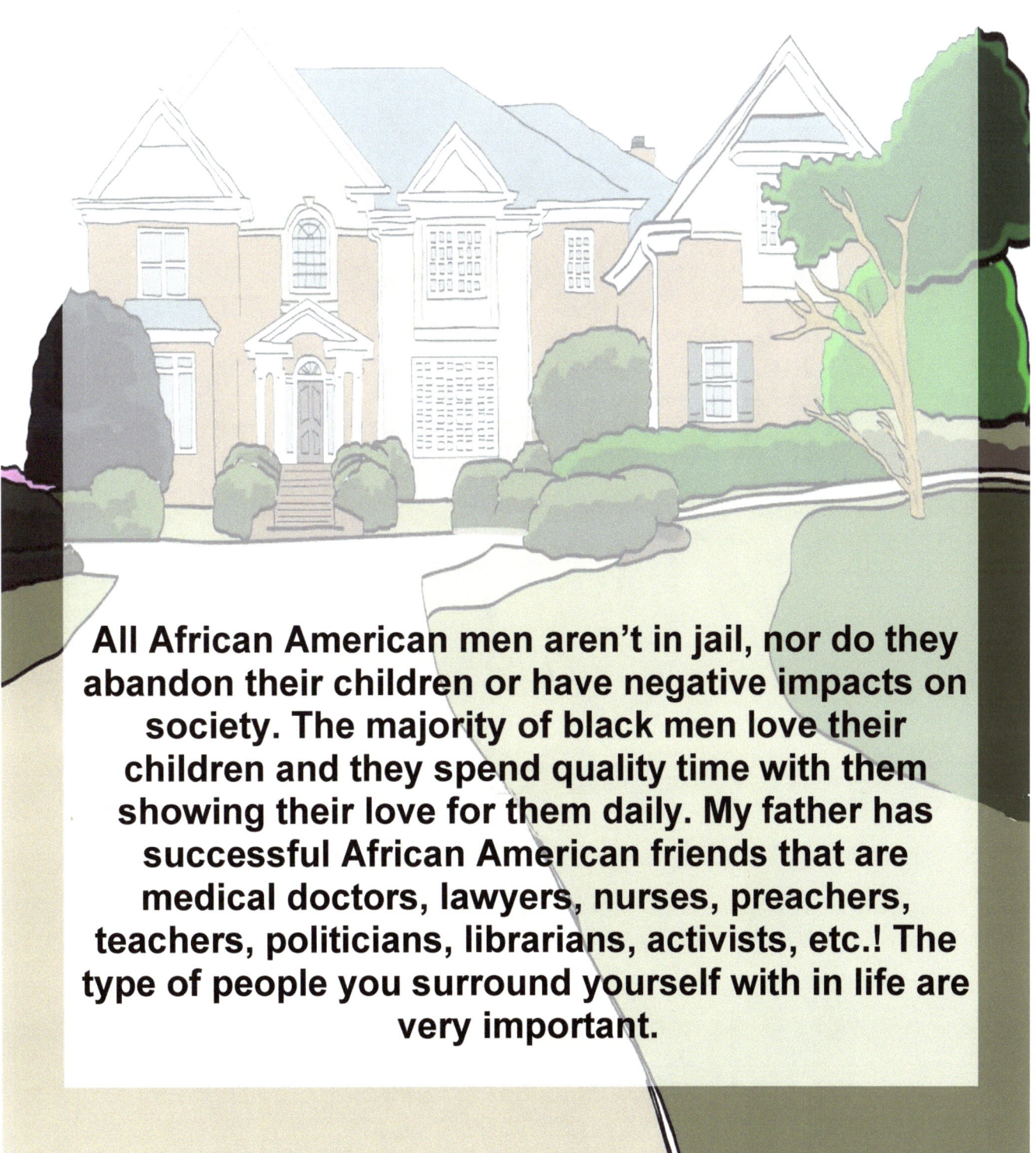

All African American men aren't in jail, nor do they abandon their children or have negative impacts on society. The majority of black men love their children and they spend quality time with them showing their love for them daily. My father has successful African American friends that are medical doctors, lawyers, nurses, preachers, teachers, politicians, librarians, activists, etc.! The type of people you surround yourself with in life are very important.

My father says that the world is made up of many different races. He says that I should always strive to uphold my own race with integrity. I love my Black friends, my White friends, my Caribbean friends, my Native American friends, my Hispanic friends, my Chinese friends, my Japanese friends, and many more! My father says that no matter what race you are, we are all equal. We are all important, and most of all, God made us all special.

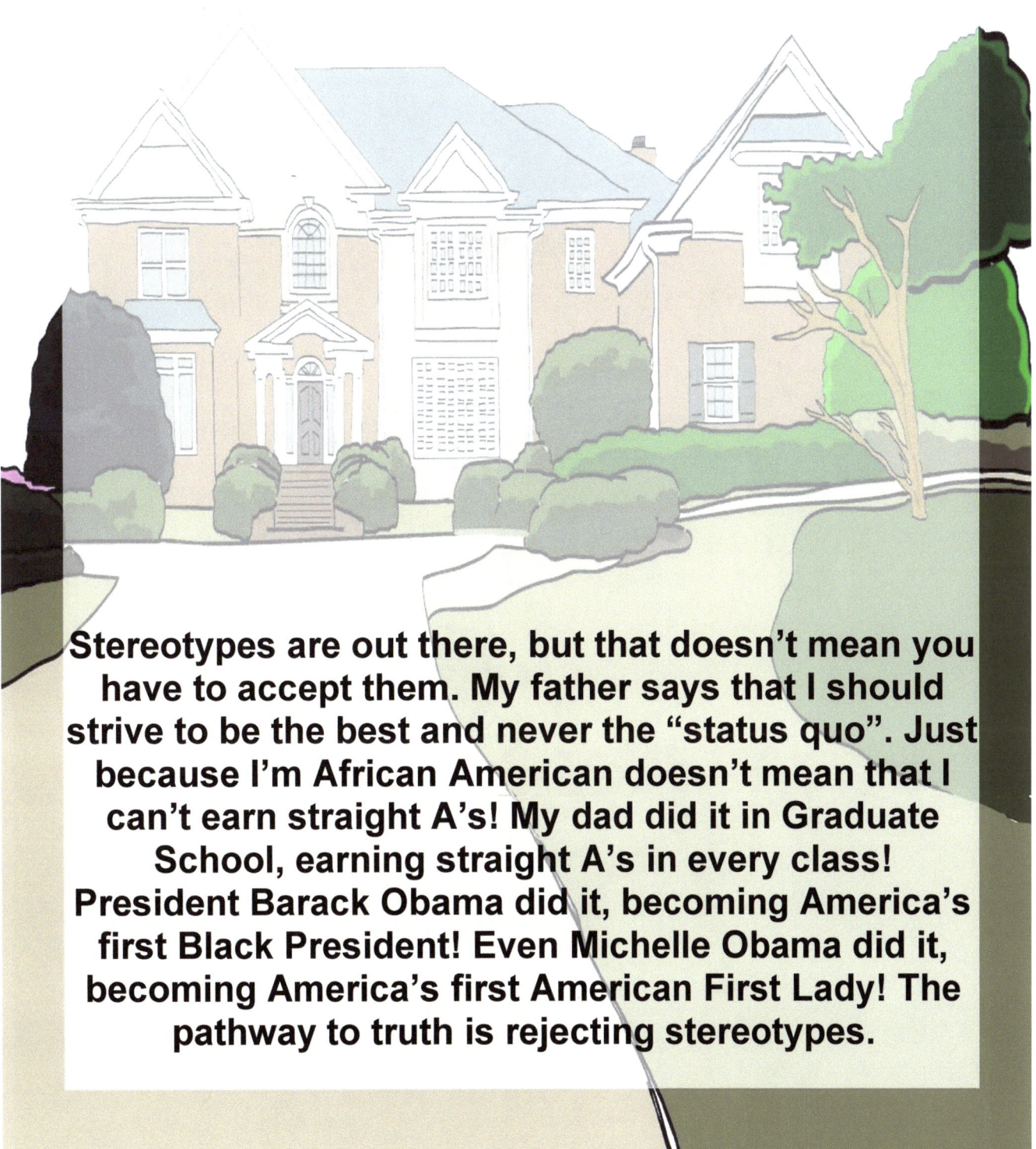

Stereotypes are out there, but that doesn't mean you have to accept them. My father says that I should strive to be the best and never the "status quo". Just because I'm African American doesn't mean that I can't earn straight A's! My dad did it in Graduate School, earning straight A's in every class! President Barack Obama did it, becoming America's first Black President! Even Michelle Obama did it, becoming America's first American First Lady! The pathway to truth is rejecting stereotypes.

The fact that I'm Black doesn't mean that I can't win the spelling bee, nor does it mean that I can't be the first person living on Mars. Yes! I said Mars! Dad says when you imagine, imagine BIG, and when someone achieves, you aim to achieve greater things! Knowledge is POWER! Dad says no matter how money or material things you have, knowledge is the only thing no one can take away from you.

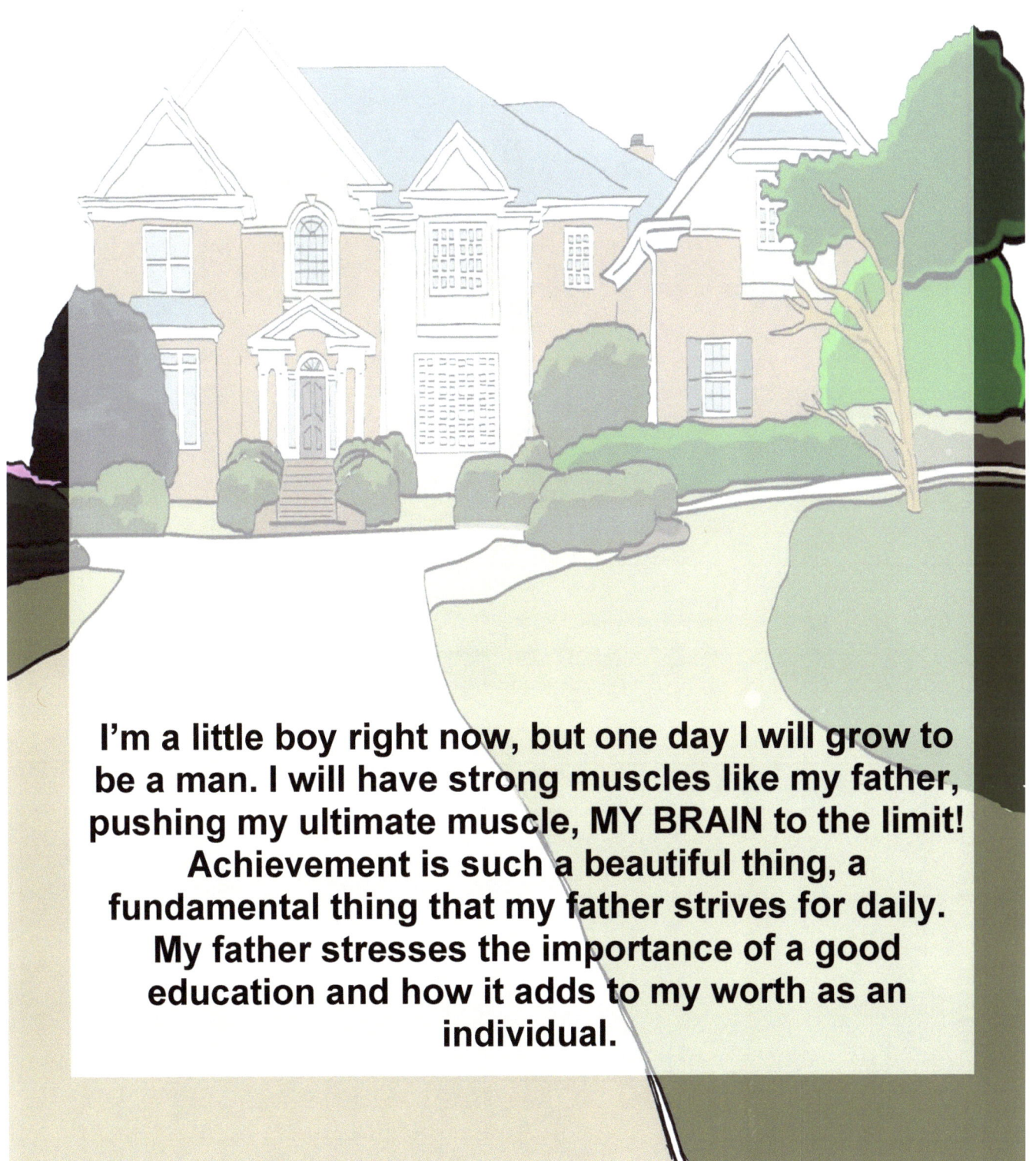

I'm a little boy right now, but one day I will grow to be a man. I will have strong muscles like my father, pushing my ultimate muscle, MY BRAIN to the limit! Achievement is such a beautiful thing, a fundamental thing that my father strives for daily. My father stresses the importance of a good education and how it adds to my worth as an individual.

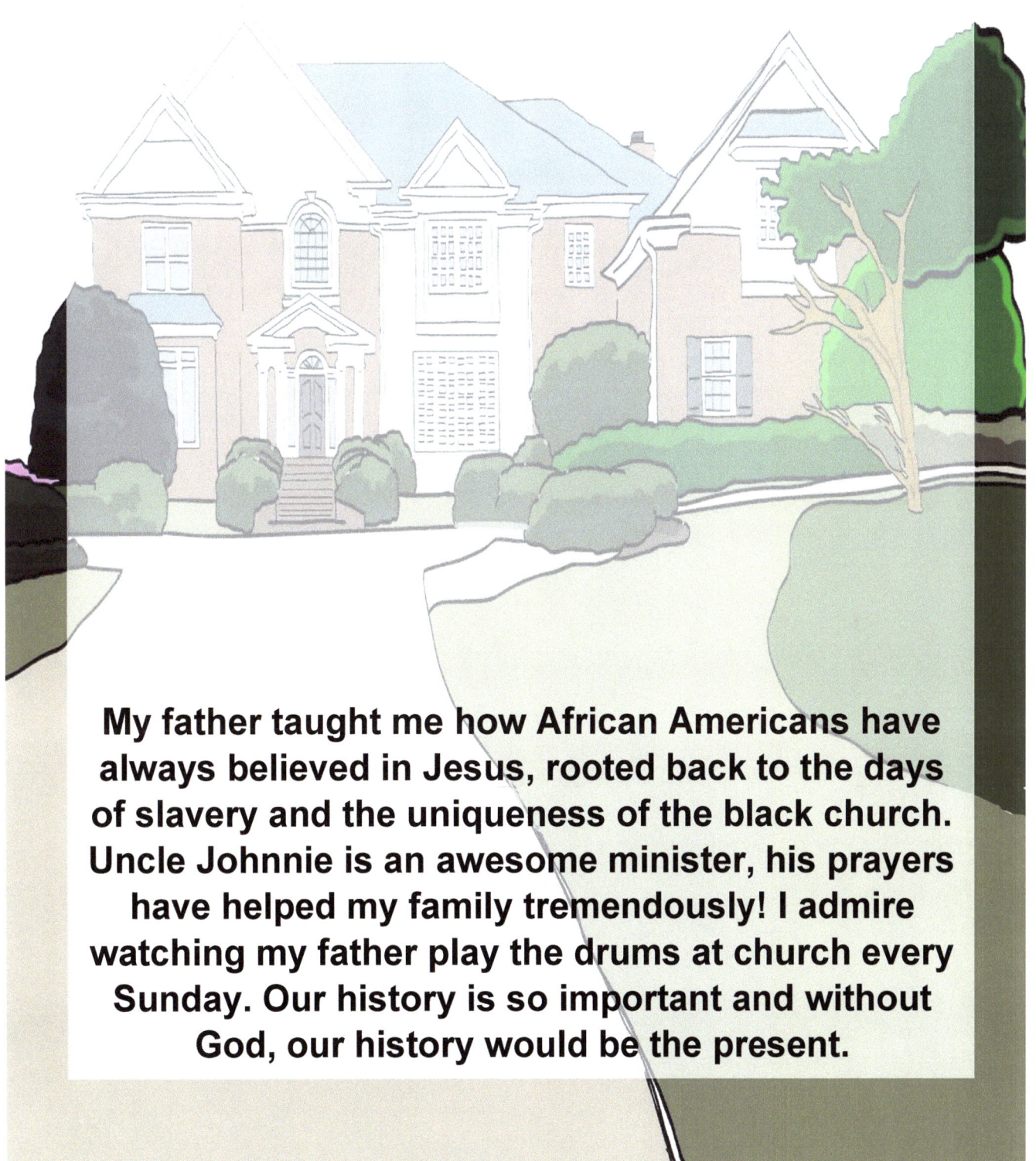

My father taught me how African Americans have always believed in Jesus, rooted back to the days of slavery and the uniqueness of the black church. Uncle Johnnie is an awesome minister, his prayers have helped my family tremendously! I admire watching my father play the drums at church every Sunday. Our history is so important and without God, our history would be the present.

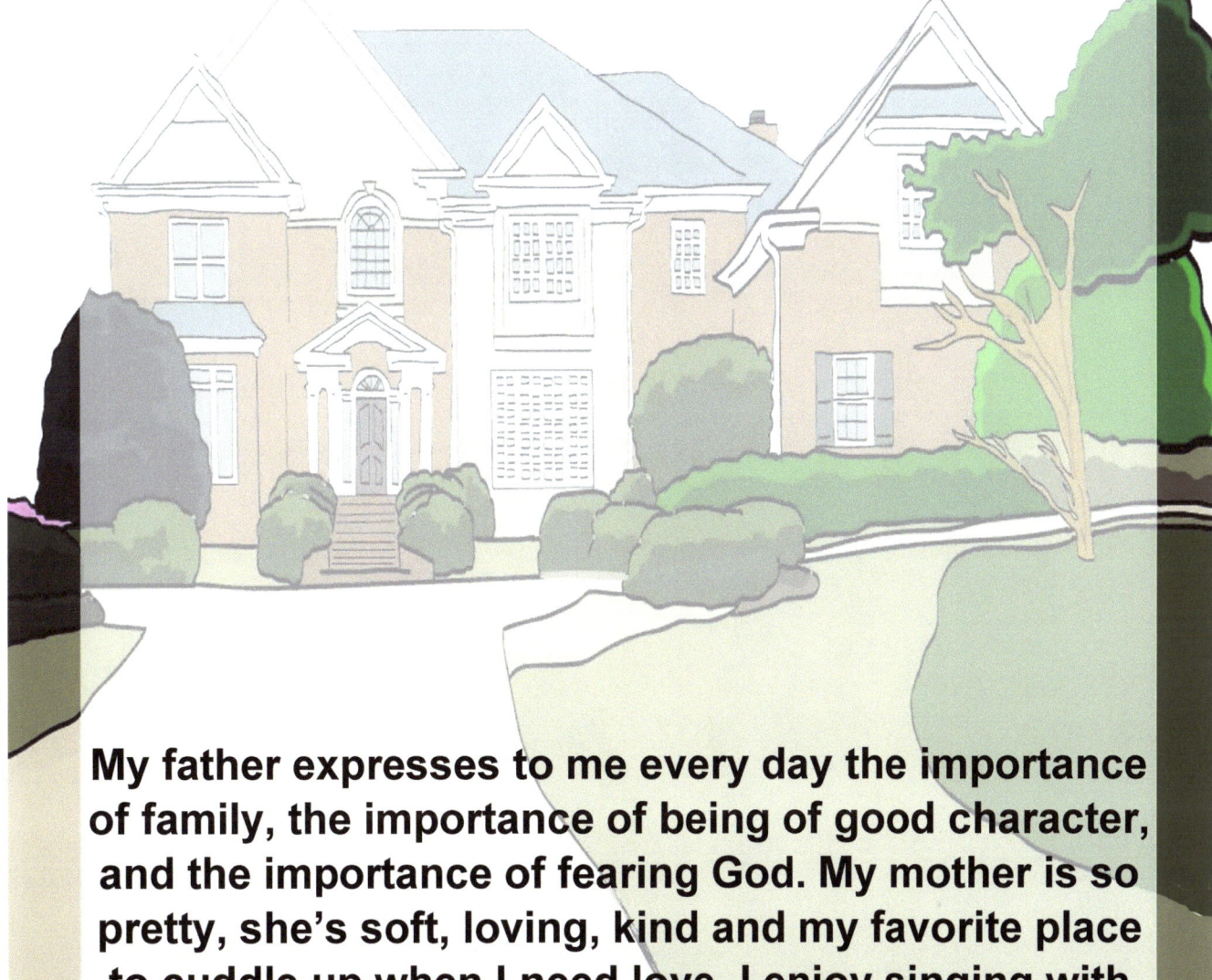

My father expresses to me every day the importance of family, the importance of being of good character, and the importance of fearing God. My mother is so pretty, she's soft, loving, kind and my favorite place to cuddle up when I need love. I enjoy singing with her "Old McDonald had a farm, E-I-E-I-O!" She's an intelligent registered nurse, so whenever I'm sick, I never have to worry! My father loves her, he makes sure she is happy and safe.

I love the way my father treats my mommy, he takes her to pretty places and she smiles a lot when she's with him. My little heart gets all warm when he cuddles with us both on the couch. Our home sweet home is full of love and happiness. We feel so safe, even our dog Prince does, too! We want for nothing because my father says all our needs have been met by God before we even ask.

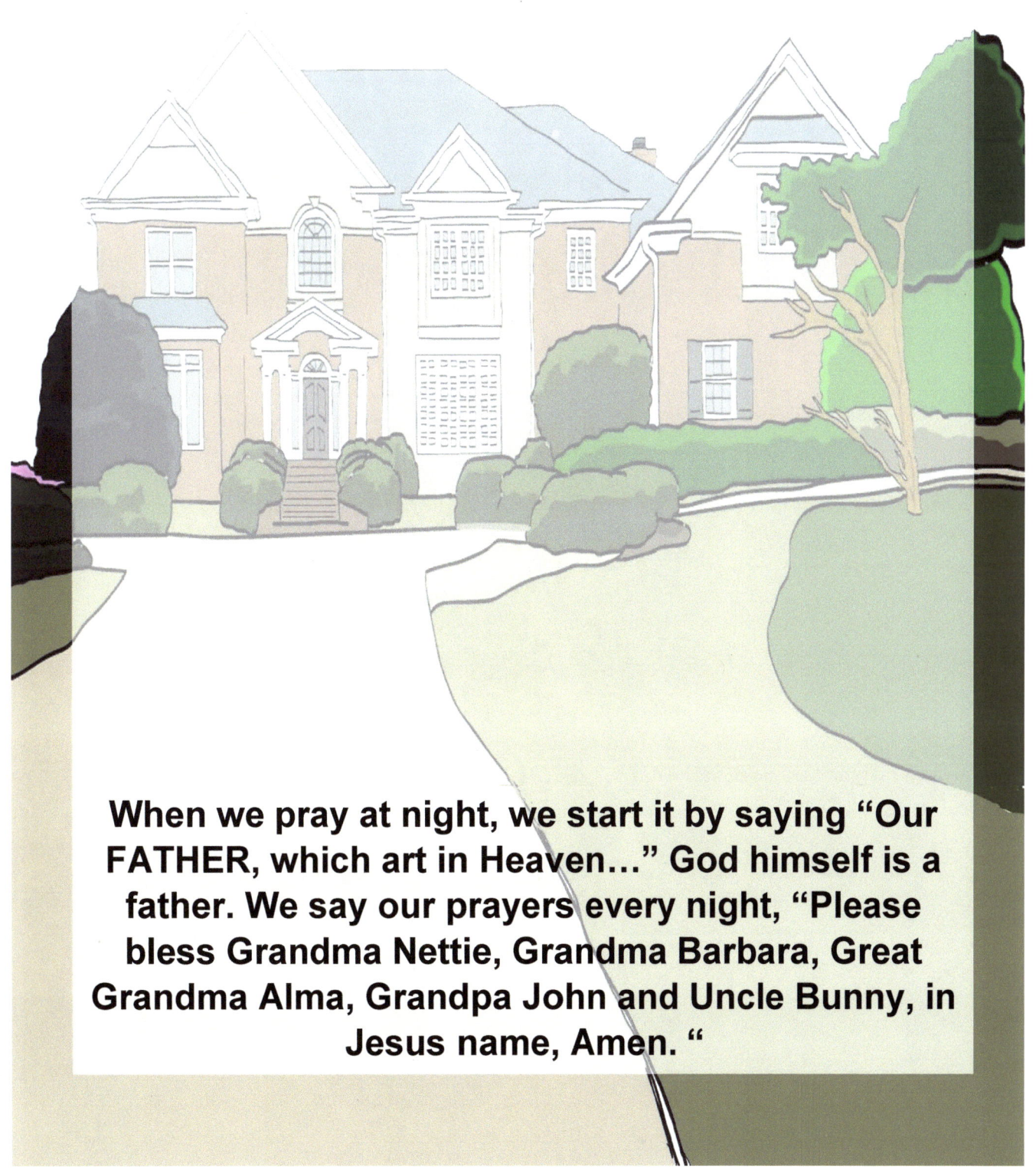

When we pray at night, we start it by saying "Our FATHER, which art in Heaven…" God himself is a father. We say our prayers every night, "Please bless Grandma Nettie, Grandma Barbara, Great Grandma Alma, Grandpa John and Uncle Bunny, in Jesus name, Amen. "

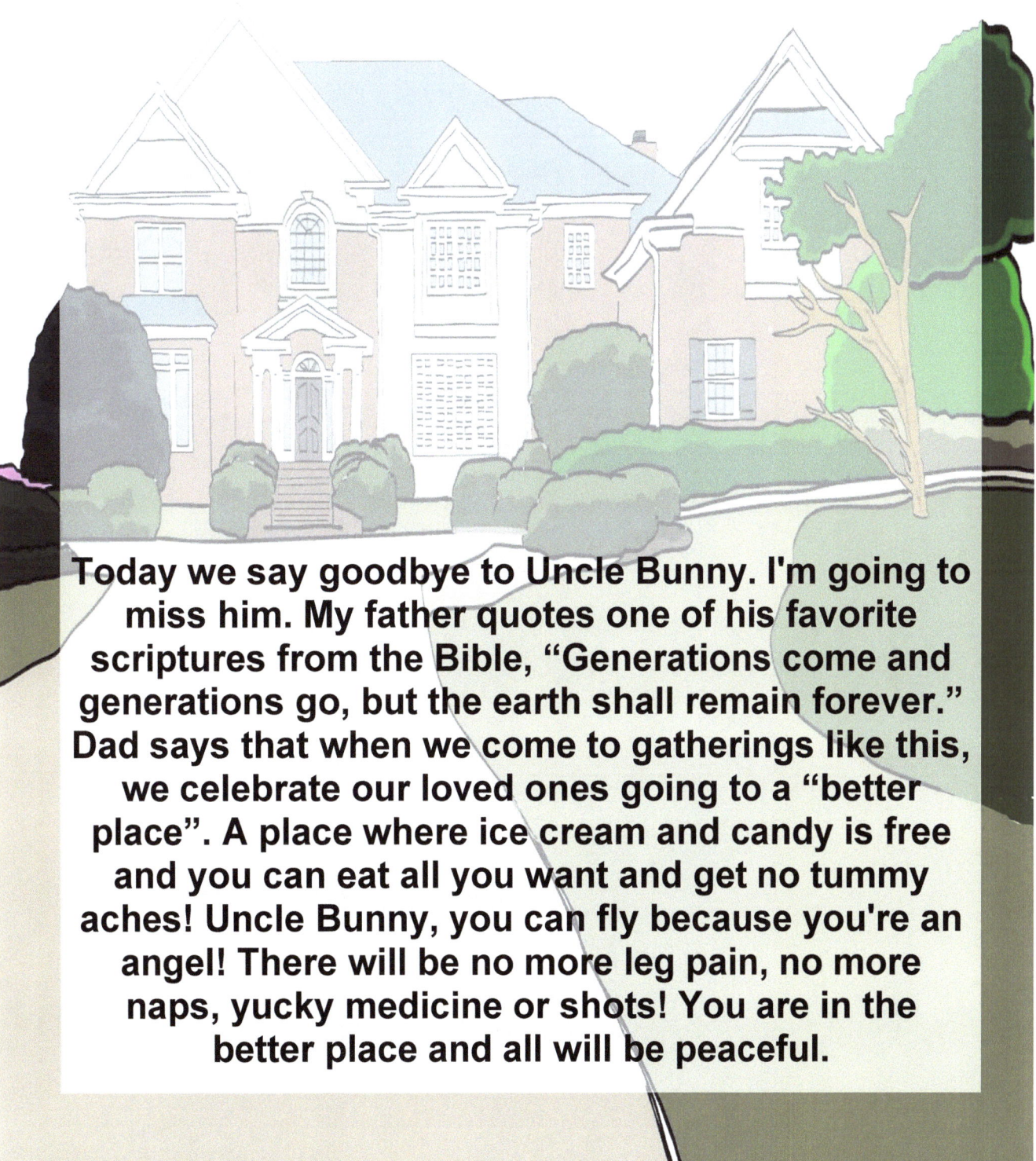

Today we say goodbye to Uncle Bunny. I'm going to miss him. My father quotes one of his favorite scriptures from the Bible, "Generations come and generations go, but the earth shall remain forever." Dad says that when we come to gatherings like this, we celebrate our loved ones going to a "better place". A place where ice cream and candy is free and you can eat all you want and get no tummy aches! Uncle Bunny, you can fly because you're an angel! There will be no more leg pain, no more naps, yucky medicine or shots! You are in the better place and all will be peaceful.

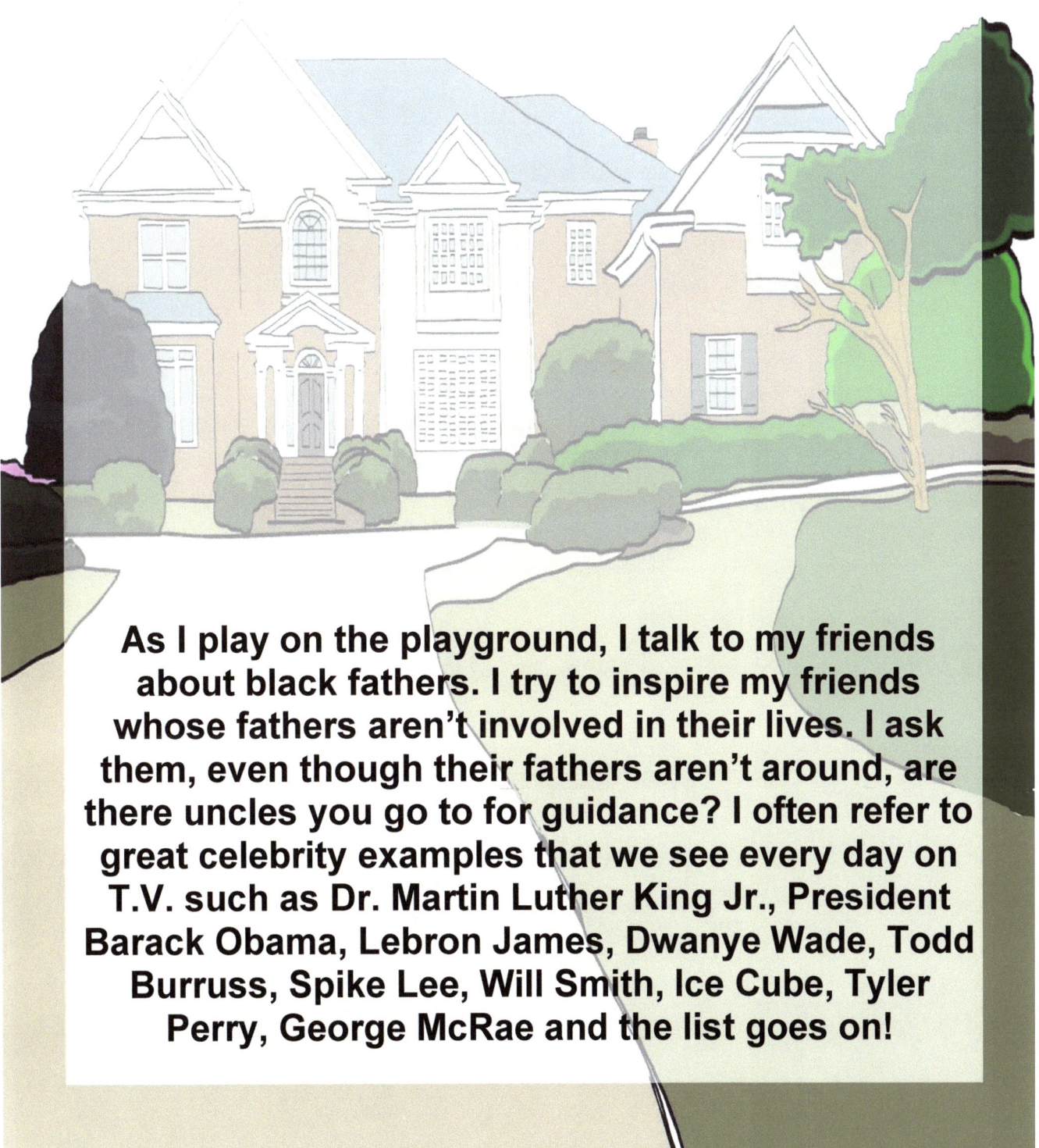

As I play on the playground, I talk to my friends about black fathers. I try to inspire my friends whose fathers aren't involved in their lives. I ask them, even though their fathers aren't around, are there uncles you go to for guidance? I often refer to great celebrity examples that we see every day on T.V. such as Dr. Martin Luther King Jr., President Barack Obama, Lebron James, Dwanye Wade, Todd Burruss, Spike Lee, Will Smith, Ice Cube, Tyler Perry, George McRae and the list goes on!

whitetail NEM $39.07 $44.32 $5.25 13.4% ABX $29.52 $35.10 $5.58 18.9% 16.2%
Sandstock ACI $16.30 $18.34 $2.04 12.5% PNC $38.45 $44.79 $6.34 16.5% 14.5%
G_Ho GOOG $918.16 $930.80 -$8.84 -0.95% UNG $13.72 $17.46 $3.74 27.3% 13.5%
Mr. Winky FB $168.71 $169.36 -$0.93 0.55% TIE $7.33 $8.24 $0.91 12.4% 10.7%
Tiptopptrader AMZN $958.00 $962.00 -$8.90 -0.92% PNK $12.71 $12.52 -$0.19 1.5% 9.3%
foss DG $76.33 $76.41 -$0.13 0.17% AN $17.68 $15.92 $1.76 10.0% 9.0%
Inqubus ESEA $5.64 $5.25 -$0.39 6.9% HNSN $5.37 $6.68 $1.31 24.4% 8.7%
skwerl DRYS $8.78 $6.99 -$1.79 20.4% FAZ $8.36 $5.42 $2.94 35.2% 7.4%
Finance CSIQ $7.60 $8.23 $0.63 8.3% UYM $17.44 $18.36 $0.92 5.3% 6.8%
Stawkryda88 XIDE $5.70 $5.96 DNDN $22.01 $20.19 $1.82 8.3% 6.4%
i_am_so_siri SLT $9.31 $9.78 DDRX $9.20 $9.89 $0.69 7.5% 6.3%
aphidh AGU $46.51 $46.05 LXU $11.97 $13.57 13.4% 6.2%
MoneyShaker GOOG $398.17 $399.01 SRS $24.32 $21.58 5.7%
mouserman HD $26.14 $24.64 CCJ $24.70 $26.09 5.7%
SkiMan721 SD $9.03 $10.55 MF $6.29 5.0%
Alaskan Frontier MEE $19.27 $21.13 RGR $11.80 4.4%
Deepfried AMR $5.37 $5.26 ALK $17.72 4.2%
56txvwoval CENX $6.10 $0.00 3.4%
JWSchmidt3 WPO $367.58 $38.70 2.1%
BranRx F $5.90 $7.85 1.8%
cactus AEM $45.23 $26.24 1.8%
Acegraphix DELL $11.99
LPNT $25.90
LVS $8.32
CEDC $23.99
CRM $41.97
MSFT $20.39
LEN $9.73
$10.01
$60.18
$16.96
$176.75
$5.43
$52.05
$30.82
$21.16
$8.32
$6.72
$6.80
$18.54 $8.47
$6.69 $18.25 -7.6%
$24.32 $127.51 -8.7%
$181.83 $70.00 -9.6%
$5.73 $110.06 -14.7%
$57.28 $14.16 -18.4%

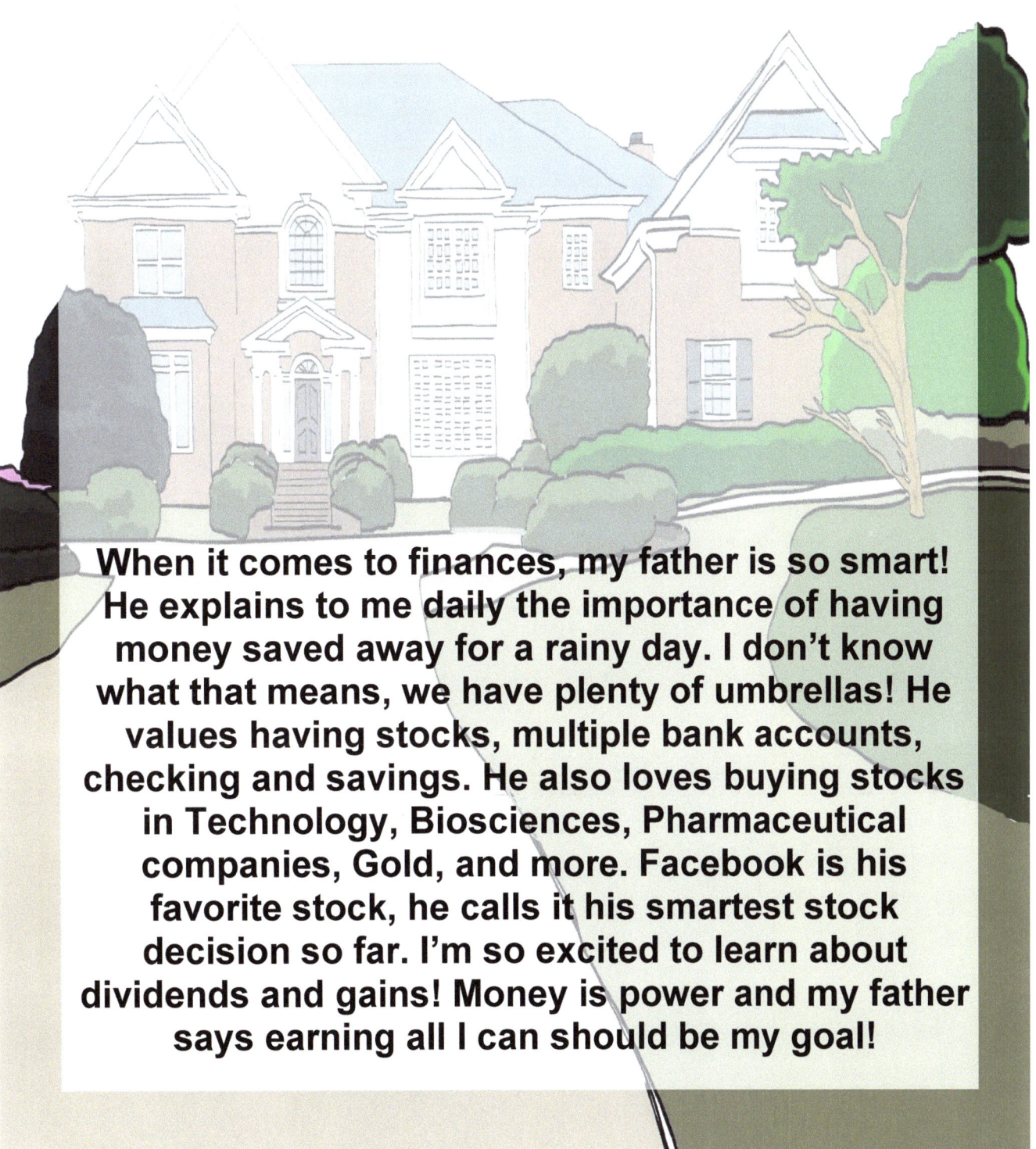

When it comes to finances, my father is so smart! He explains to me daily the importance of having money saved away for a rainy day. I don't know what that means, we have plenty of umbrellas! He values having stocks, multiple bank accounts, checking and savings. He also loves buying stocks in Technology, Biosciences, Pharmaceutical companies, Gold, and more. Facebook is his favorite stock, he calls it his smartest stock decision so far. I'm so excited to learn about dividends and gains! Money is power and my father says earning all I can should be my goal!

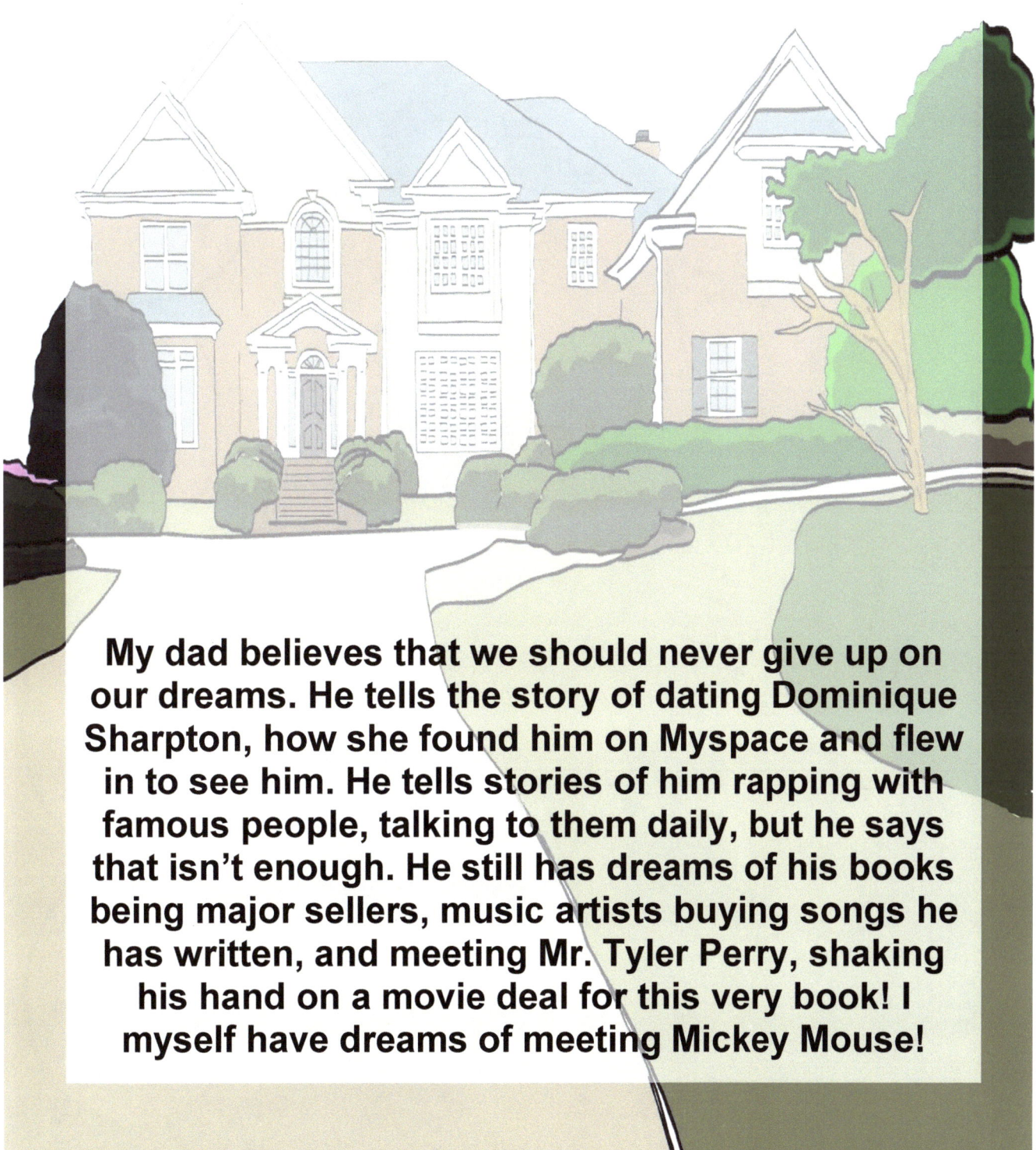

My dad believes that we should never give up on our dreams. He tells the story of dating Dominique Sharpton, how she found him on Myspace and flew in to see him. He tells stories of him rapping with famous people, talking to them daily, but he says that isn't enough. He still has dreams of his books being major sellers, music artists buying songs he has written, and meeting Mr. Tyler Perry, shaking his hand on a movie deal for this very book! I myself have dreams of meeting Mickey Mouse!

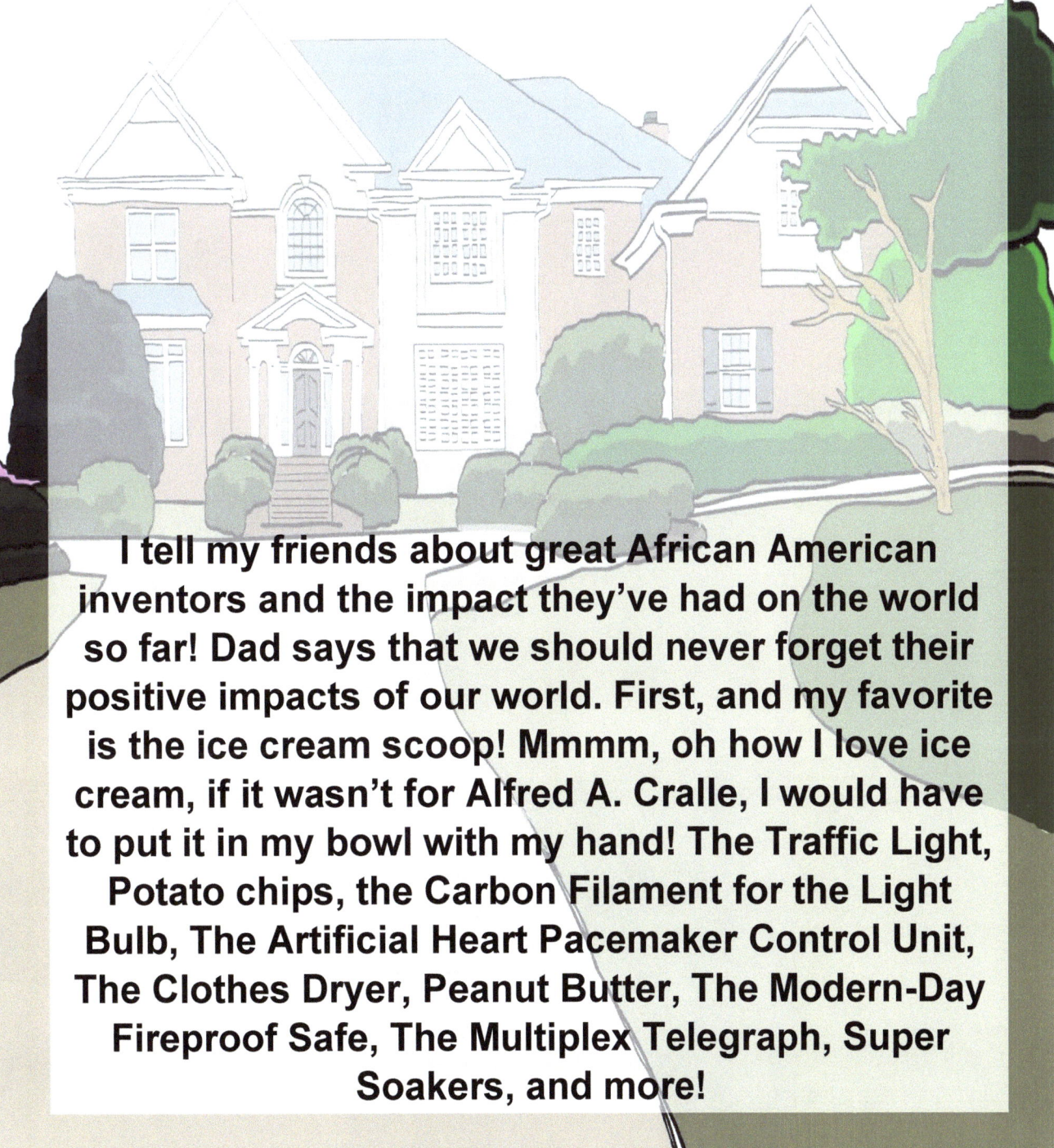

I tell my friends about great African American inventors and the impact they've had on the world so far! Dad says that we should never forget their positive impacts of our world. First, and my favorite is the ice cream scoop! Mmmm, oh how I love ice cream, if it wasn't for Alfred A. Cralle, I would have to put it in my bowl with my hand! The Traffic Light, Potato chips, the Carbon Filament for the Light Bulb, The Artificial Heart Pacemaker Control Unit, The Clothes Dryer, Peanut Butter, The Modern-Day Fireproof Safe, The Multiplex Telegraph, Super Soakers, and more!

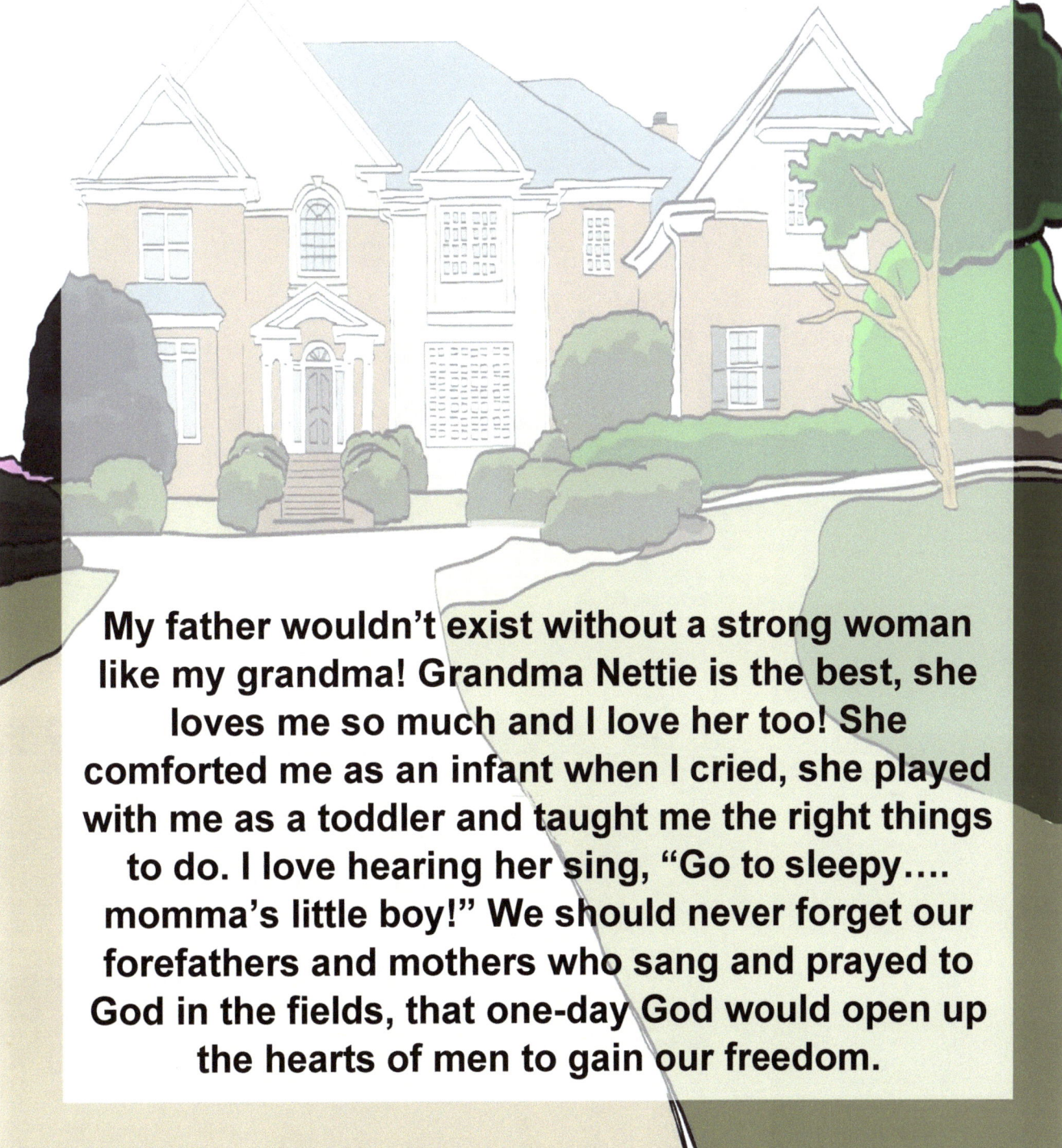

My father wouldn't exist without a strong woman like my grandma! Grandma Nettie is the best, she loves me so much and I love her too! She comforted me as an infant when I cried, she played with me as a toddler and taught me the right things to do. I love hearing her sing, "Go to sleepy…. momma's little boy!" We should never forget our forefathers and mothers who sang and prayed to God in the fields, that one-day God would open up the hearts of men to gain our freedom.

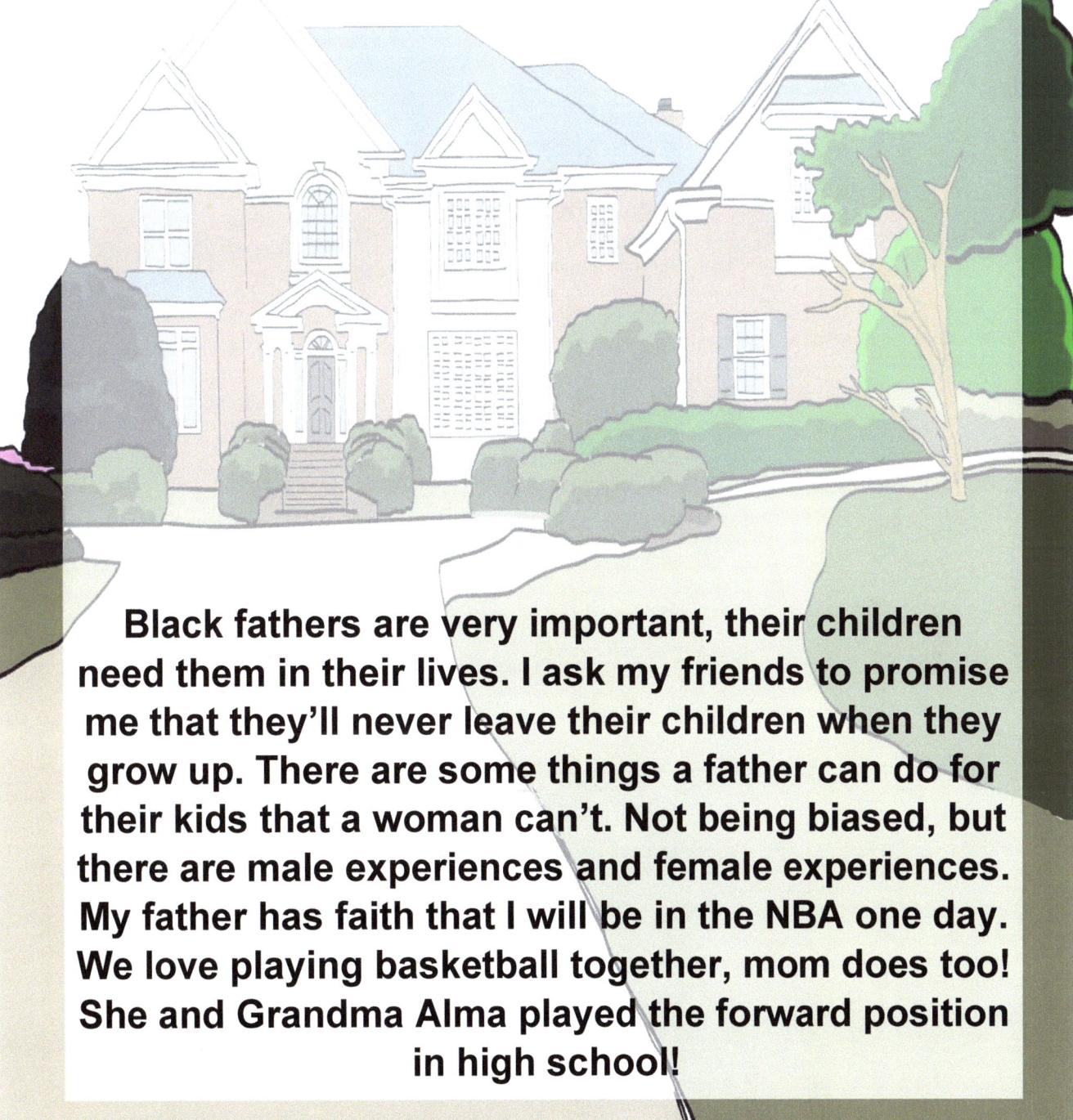

Black fathers are very important, their children need them in their lives. I ask my friends to promise me that they'll never leave their children when they grow up. There are some things a father can do for their kids that a woman can't. Not being biased, but there are male experiences and female experiences. My father has faith that I will be in the NBA one day. We love playing basketball together, mom does too! She and Grandma Alma played the forward position in high school!

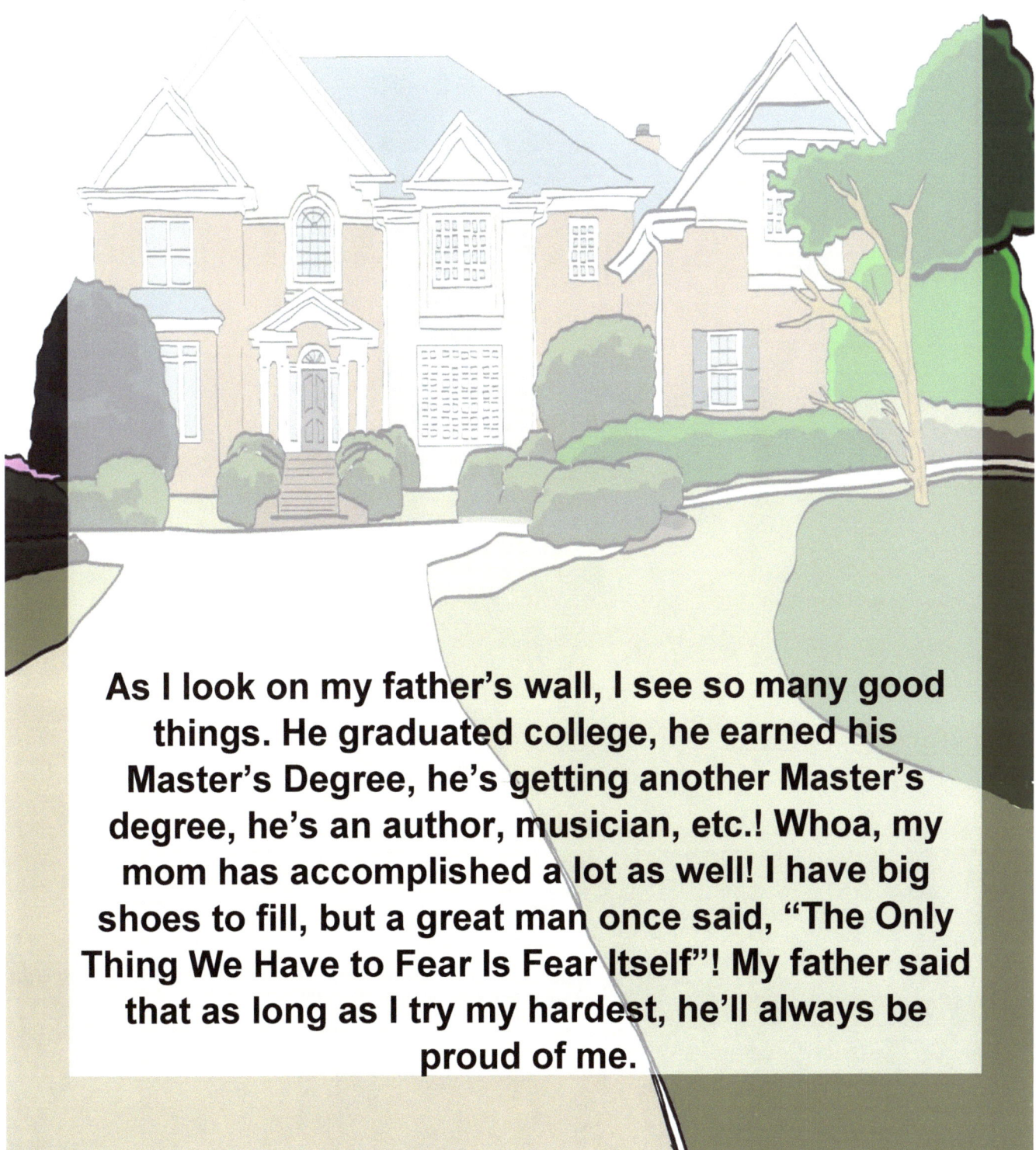

As I look on my father's wall, I see so many good things. He graduated college, he earned his Master's Degree, he's getting another Master's degree, he's an author, musician, etc.! Whoa, my mom has accomplished a lot as well! I have big shoes to fill, but a great man once said, "The Only Thing We Have to Fear Is Fear Itself"! My father said that as long as I try my hardest, he'll always be proud of me.

Soon, I'll be sharing my toys with my little sister Brianna! She's so beautiful, she's so precious! Mommy and Daddy are so excited today, our family has grown again! When Brianna was born, dad ran through the hospital yelling, "The Princess Is Here!" My father has trust funds for us both already, because Proverbs 13:22 says that's what a real man does!

So, I end by saying, you know me as Camren, an African American boy full of potential! Black fathers are very much needed. Every black man should be determined to change the current stereotype. When you see a black child walking with their father, think of Cam. When you see a black father braiding his little girl's hair, think of Bri. Most importantly, when you want change, think of YOURSELF, the power is in you!

Author's Note

First and foremost, I'd like to thank God the Father and his son Jesus, for blessing me with the talents to express myself. Secondly, thank God for making this book a reality. Next, I would like to thank the amazingly beautiful mother of my children Kellye', for bringing them into the world, being a loving mother and blessing me with two beautiful, incredible blessings. Also, to Monya Tomlinson for proofreading my work, Aaron Archie for his amazing illustrations, William Lee and Lee's Press for believing in my work. I wrote this book to express to millions around our world that all black men do not desert their children. All children with black dads aren't negatively influenced, but to be a FATHER is so much more than being a dad. Black Fathers Are Real, We Do Exist. It was my parents who provided the unconditional love and nurture that would anchor my lifelong process of learning, loving, caring for others, educating others and forever aspiring to be the best in all that I do. I inspire my two children to be the best in EVERYTHING that they do and never forgetting to give positive attributes back to society. As the son of an African American man, my father passed away at the age of 12 years old, but he was a great example of what a black father is. He was a teacher, a provider, a protector, present daily, a pillar of strength, support and discipline.

Thank you to everyone who supports, loves, and believes in me.

May God Bless You.